Aspire

The Beginnings of the Canaan Trust

by

Dean Anderson

© Copyright 2019 Dean Anderson

All rights reserved.

No part of this publication may be reproduced, stored in a retrieval system, or transmitted, in any form or by any means, electronic, mechanical, photocopying, recording or otherwise, without the prior written permission of the publisher.

British Library Cataloguing in Publication Data.

A catalogue record for this book is available from the British Library

ISBN 978 0 86071 810 9

A Commissioned Publication Printed by
MOORLEYS
Print, Design & Publishing
info@moorleys.co.uk · www.moorleys.co.uk

Contents

Foreword	i
Introduction	ii
Chapter 1 – The Meadows	1
Chapter 2 – The Oasis	5
Chapter 3 – The Jacket	9
Chapter 4 – The Shed	13
Chapter 5 – The Park	15
Chapter 6 – The Challenge	19
Chapter 7 – Fading Summer 1995	23
Chapter 8 – Aspire	27
Chapter 9 – The Springboard	31

Foreword

'Lord, when did we see you hungry and feed you, or thirsty and give you something to drink? When did we see you a stranger and invite you in, or needing clothes and clothe you?"
Matthew 25:37-38

2020 will mark 25 years since the creation of the Aspire Trust which later became the Canaan Trust. The Aspire Trust came into being following an amazing act of Christian charity by The Anderson Family. This is Dean's story of how that decision came to be made and how it inspired others to action.

With typical generosity they have covered the costs of this print run so that until 31st December 2020 every penny you have paid for this book will go to the ongoing work of the Canaan Trust. After that date 50% of the profits will come to Canaan as the family support other worthy causes.

Sadly the last 25 years has seen homelessness rise not diminish, Canaan is supporting more people than ever with accommodation, food parcels, advice, a listening ear. We do not see next year as one of celebration rather one of thanksgiving that people like yourselves are prepared to answer the call to help and support those in need.

We appreciate that our supporters come from many faiths and backgrounds but as Trustees we are always mindful that we are a Christian based project attempting to do His work here in Erewash and Broxtowe. Whenever a need has been identified prayer has been answered and solutions or resources have come forward.

As we move into the next 25 years and the unknown challenges that will present themselves we do so inspired by Dean's story and in confidence that with your continued support and faith in the Lord we will together be able to answer the call of the hungry, the thirsty, the stranger.

The Trustees
September 2019

Introduction

Robert Brian Anderson married Faith Westwick on the 24th September 1960 at the Parish Church in Lenton, Nottingham.

They'd both grown up locally, Robert in Dunkirk and Faith in Lenton.

Their lives had not been easy up to that point, Robert was brought up by mum with seven other siblings.

Dad had passed away years before and now, as one of six lads, he would find himself coal picking on the railway or having to borrow his sister's swimming costume to swim in the local quarry pool.

Faith was born in September 1939 and had grown up with the knowledge that her parents hadn't really wanted her, whether because of the start of the war, whether because they'd wanted a son or any other reason, she felt rejected, only finding strength with her older sister Margaret and younger brother Fred.

As the war progressed and came to its conclusion, the Westwick family life was to change forever.

The injuries and trauma sustained by dad meant that the family would be torn apart and divorce was on the horizon.

With the ongoing love and support of Margaret and Fred, Faith would spend little time at home. She joined a local church and it wasn't long before Faith by name was matched by her enthusiasm for her new found faith.

Her brokenness was now being channelled into serving others and, she believed, serving God.

With great enthusiasm she would ride her bicycle to wherever the next mission meeting was, including Sandiacre and Long Eaton. She loved her new found family and would do anything to help the church progress. Relationships that were being built at this time would last her lifetime.

Having met Robert Brian, who became affectionately known as Brian, she began a new family trying to put the hurt of the past behind her, starting afresh.

In November 1961 their first son was born. Dean Michael. Dean after the singer Dean Martin and Michael after the archangel Michael. An interesting mix!

They lived with Faith's sister Margaret and husband Ken on Mettham Street in Lenton due to them not being able to afford a place of their own.

Theirs would have been a homeless start if it hadn't been for the help of family.

Sadly, within a few months their son had been diagnosed with double pneumonia. The news was devastating but together they prayed that Dean would pull through. They made promises to God that if their son would survive, if his life was spared then they as parents would bring him up in the ways of God through Jesus Christ.

Dean was christened at the same Parish Church where Faith and Brian had married and it seemed as though God had heard and granted their request.

In later life they would speak fondly of how the family helped them at a time when they needed a place to live. Even at that early point they could have found themselves homeless.

Chapter 1 - The Meadows

I got back from the team leader's meeting, sort of excited but definitely nervous. Nervous about the proposition, nervous about Lynnette's reaction, nervous for Michael and Nathan our lads.
The Nottingham project needed someone or some people to take it on. Neil and his family had given it their all for many years and now was the time for them to move on.
I sat down with Lynnette and we talked about the meeting.
'The Meadows!' she exclaimed
'You want us as a family to look after the church project on The Meadows?'
My nervous feeling had proved right, but I knew that she would seriously think about it and more importantly pray.
Michael was six and Nathan was four. They straight away were enthusiastic when I mentioned the Friday night Youth Club and my quickly made up ideas for our short term appointment.
The team leader, David, was sure that it would be a short term appointment and assured us that we would have the full support of the Beeston congregation.
We were welcomed by The Meadows congregation and local community project workers and there we began what turned out to be two years of joy, tears, hard, yet rewarding work, rewarding beyond words!
After much thought and prayer our friends, Karen and Wayne, decided to join us in the main bulk of work along with a couple of university students, Andy and Ruth. They supported us on a Friday night with our youth project.
We were and continue to be eternally grateful for the hard work, commitment and sacrifice that they, along with the rest of the congregation put into this church and community project on The Meadows.

Our journey in life had taken an unexpected turn and our progress to this lovely part of Nottingham was helping us to work in a team, to trust those people around us, but more importantly, to trust God who we believed we were serving.

One Friday night in the Spring of 1991, after about a year of working in The Meadows, one of our young people who came every Friday night without fail had a disagreement with another Youth Club member. He then went on to have a further disagreement with one of our staff team. At this point we had to, for his own safety and the safety of other Youth Club members, encourage him to go home.
I knew that as soon as he ran down Bathley Street towards home we were in for a challenging evening.
I left other members of staff in charge whilst I waited outside St Faith's, our big old church building.
It was only a few minutes before I heard the screeching of tyres, banging car doors and then being surrounded by our Youth Club member's older brothers.
They stood around me, all of them seemed at least six inches taller than my five foot nine and a half inches.
They demanded to know what had happened to their brother at our Youth Club.
Apparently he was sat on the floor sobbing at home.
He loved coming on a Friday night.
I started to explain what had happened but quickly moved on to the reasons why we were doing what we were doing on a Friday night, in fact the reasons why we were in The Meadows full stop.
As soon as I mentioned Jesus Christ the three of them backed off and started using words like 'respect'.
My heartbeat having raced seemed at this point to be settling down a little.
I told them that in two weeks their brother would be welcomed back with a clean slate and we'd start again.

Before the three got back into their Montego car they thanked me for what I was doing and they were going back to straighten their brother out.

I shouted not to be too hard on him as their car pulled quietly onto Bathley Street.

I raised my head to heaven to say thank you as Wayne appeared at the big oak church door.

The project on a daily basis served the community with luncheon club, toddlers, church community services, and OAP visitation schemes. It was a real joy working with other churches and community groups who shared the same and sometimes even greater enthusiasm than we had for the area.

For two years we gave it our all and felt as though the people who lived around Bathley Street and further afield appreciated our efforts in what we were trying to achieve.

Ours wasn't the only project in that area of Nottingham with many other church and community groups working together and meeting together to best serve this great city.

In the Spring of 1992 we didn't realise that our journey as a family was about to take a different turn, and a turn that I certainly was not expecting.

There was a Rectory next to St Faith's church building and I really believed at the beginning of 1992 that we as a family would move there.

The work was, in my opinion, progressing, and we had other ideas about how we wanted to see other projects come to fruition.

Our Monday morning team leader's meeting in Beeston was about to deliver a shock. A decision had been made that the church project on The Meadows was to finish and that we as a family would need to consider a different path.

At first I felt that this was a wrong decision. I talked to the team about my thoughts and plans and that I'd expected us to move into the Rectory that spring and The Meadows would become our home.
After another week all was confirmed and I was asked to come to another team meeting with Lynnette.
The team leader asked us if we would consider working alongside Michael in our home town of Long Eaton. I knew of the positive way the church was growing there and now we were being asked to serve in this new situation.
We went away to think, to talk, to pray and in the late Spring of 1992 we started our work with the team in Long Eaton.
One thing I was certain of was that our lives wouldn't be so manic and things would settle down a little for us as a family.
How wrong I was!
I met with church and community leaders on The Meadows for one last time and told them that they would certainly be in our thoughts and prayers and that I would come back over to see how different projects were progressing.
I felt sad after leaving this meeting but a sense inside that this was the right step.

St Faith's

Chapter 2 - The Oasis

The Long Eaton church project, known as The Oasis was already in full swing. Growth was rapid after years of difficulty and decline.

The Oasis

Michael was from the Rhondda in South Wales and with all his Welsh enthusiasm and the support of David the team leader, we were seeing something unusual, a church that was growing!

After a period of settling and adjustment, [about a week or so], we were asked if we would engage in youth work as part of the church project outreach and to look after the young people of families that came to the church.

At first I felt despondent, having worked with children and young people since 1979 I really did think that it was time for a change. In fact a change would have been nice.

But I was reminded at this point of words that someone had said to both Lynnette and myself in the past.

It went something like this:

'Get on with what's in front of you and when the time comes to do something different that then will become clear'.

So as a couple we sat down and agreed that if our parents would help with looking after Michael and Nathan then we would take on the youth work.

Our minds and hearts had now started to settle for The Meadows and our passion for serving the community, inspired by our faith in God was about to be re-directed to our home town.

Straight away we had lots of volunteers who were keen to get involved in the youth work, and this wasn't surprising with the church growth and people genuinely wanting to serve the community because of their new found faith and, for others, their reinvigorated faith. Ian, Tony and Stuart amongst many others.

Our first job was to get the young people together who were already part of the church. We began weekly activities both fun and practical and also devotional.

One particular Thursday evening stands out in my memory. It was Maundy Thursday and the young people had arranged stations around the church building on Derby Road to mark out the progression of the Easter story. I was excited but also humbled watching them express faith in this modern world.

Some of those who organised this would go on to join the youth team and be instrumental in growing this youth work.
Much followed including taking assemblies in fifteen local schools, and in some of those schools we organised after school clubs.
What an enthusiastic team we had, Carl, Carolyn, [who would go on to get married]
Laura and others.
At Cloudside Junior School in Sandiacre we held an after school club and we organised a Tuesday early evening children's church.
As we had such a great team of volunteers, the scope of youth work continued to grow on site and in the community.
We were known locally as the 'Ofsted Assembly Team' due to the high demand for assemblies whenever inspections were taking place.
We knew that not every teacher appreciated our enthusiastic style but many did including those headteachers who asked us time and time again to take assemblies and lessons.
I remember one particular assembly at a secondary school in the town. We played a rap song that was all about prayer and the look on those young people's faces as Carl struck up the song Wonderwall by Oasis.
'How could a team from a local church make assemblies so appealing?' I heard one teacher say to her colleague.
I loved working with the local schools and this would prove to be an invaluable relationship.

Chapter 3 - The Jacket

The church building was right next to King Street and King Street was one of the main access streets to Long Eaton's famous park, West Park.

The Jacket

Hundreds of young people in any one week would walk down King Street.

Autumn 1992 would see a celebration event aimed at those young people and being organised by the youth team.
It simply would be called 'Youth Festival' and was going to be aimed at engaging with those passing young people.
Drama, music, activities and a Sunday night concert were all planned. The team were keen to let those young people know that the church was there for them as it was there for any other age group in the community.
November 1992 over the three nights we saw over a hundred young people come in and experience our first Youth Festival.
All was going well until the Sunday night when, naively, we joined our 6pm service with the finale of the Youth Festival.
Our congregation were in for a bit of a shock. Everything was going well. A team had come over from Nottingham and were delivering great music, drama and David was now speaking.
We'd known David from our time in Nottingham where he was Youth Director at a thriving city centre church.
He was very supportive of local churches and their youth programmes, giving of his time generously.
His lively talk wasn't going to be long but a small group of lads decided that they weren't wanting to listen.
They had been every night to this point but now with colourful language they were making their intentions clear in front of a packed church. I quietly told them that I wanted them to stay but they weren't in agreement with my terms.
It was now my dubious pleasure to organise for them to leave the building and in this process one of the lads whose name was Rickie had his jacket ripped as we made it outside.
This was the point where he now was going to break every window in the building and was going to sue me for damage to his jacket.
I was glad to see that among two or three congregation members who had followed us out my dad was among them. They were praying

quietly and I turned to Rickie put my hand on his head and prayed for him.
He became quiet and my heart settled down.
Alan, one of the church members who had followed us out, pushed forty pounds into my hand and in Rickie's hearing said to go out and buy him a new jacket.
I met him at 10am the following day and we went out and bought a new jacket.

The Youth Festival was seen as a great success with many new young people joining the church and many others getting involved in other youth activities and projects.
One of those projects became affectionately known as 'The Shed'.

Chapter 4 - The Shed

The Shed has a key role in opening up the rest of this story.
The Shed? I hear you ask.
Yes, our Friday night Youth Club became known as The Shed, but also the corrugated listed building that has been standing since the 1890's was affectionately known as The Shed.

The Shed

It stands at the back of the main church building on King Street and for us was the ideal setting for our envisaged Youth Club.
Equipment for the project quickly came together with pool tables, table tennis table, TVs to play music videos and computer games and even a pinball machine!
The word soon got round and before long The Shed was alive with young people.

One particular Friday night one of our youth club members decided to start throwing pool balls around. I asked him to stop pointing out the obvious danger that he was causing, but unfortunately, he didn't agree.
He was a big lad and at around two hundred and twenty pounds it took a few members of staff to encourage him out of the building.
Later that same night after all was packed away and we still hadn't had tea I was stopping at the chip shop on Main Street to pick up some chips.
I couldn't believe it when I saw in the small queue the lad who we had asked to leave earlier in the evening.
He spotted me straight away and went on to tell everyone in the chip shop what had happened that night. Memories of The Meadows came flooding back. But, instead of aggression, he was thanking me for what we did on a Friday night and quickly apologising for his own stupidity that evening.
I smiled at the people in the queue and he came and shook my hand. My heart settled and I looked up to heaven.
My chips seemed to taste extra good that night.

Chapter 5 - The Park

As the youth work progressed and Summer approached in 1993 the youth team talked about outreach work on West Park.
Somebody had told us that as many as a hundred young people would be hanging out on the park on any particular Friday night.
I thought that this figure must be exaggerated so the following Friday with another team member we wandered over to the park.

The Park

There was at least fifty or more just sitting around on the park near the bandstand. After brief conversations with some of the young people we recognised that they thought it was a good idea for some of the youth team to come over on a Friday evening and engage with the group of young people.
Again, because of the great team we had, we managed to start our outreach work.
Part of that work was making sure that young people were safe going home off the park and sometimes we would be there until 11pm.

Late Spring 1995 was again one of those periods of time where things were about to change.
We'd noticed that a small group of lads were always still on the park no matter what time we left or what time the majority of young people left. Among that group there was a young man who was older than the others and he always kept his distance and wouldn't engage in any conversation. We found out that his name was Kenny and he was quite a bit older than the oldest teenagers in the group.
Most of the young people said that Kenny was alright, but others seemed quite cruel in their description of his mental health condition.
One Friday night we finally managed to engage in conversation with this small group.
I asked the question of why they always stayed when everyone else was gone.
'We sleep on the park'.
At first I thought they meant that they fell asleep on the park and then went home.
No.
They slept on the park, they slept in skips, they slept in doorways, wherever they could get most comfortable that was their bed for the night.

I was shocked. Maybe I was naive to think that the homeless problem was reserved for the cities and here in my town I have lads who have no home to go to.
I didn't sleep that night. My mind was racing and I was confusingly asking God, why?

Chapter 6 - The Challenge

We had our team leaders' meetings on a Monday morning. Over the weekend before our meeting I was putting together a case for us as a church community to take action to help this group and others who we were not aware of.

I already knew that several people in the church were helping younger people with accommodation and I knew I needed to speak to them.

Monday morning came and what I blurted out right at the beginning of the meeting didn't look anything like the notes I had prepared.

My heart on the subject was laid bare.

Our meeting that Monday morning turned out to be a lengthy one.

The team tasked me with gathering information, researching the local extent of the problem and practical ways that we as a community could further help. The meeting was reminded of the many people who were already being helped in this way by members of the congregation.

With sandwich in one hand and phone in the other I began with Erewash Borough Council. The housing officer I spoke to thought it would be a good idea to meet up so we arranged an appointment.

Coffee on the table, we sat and I watched as he opened his briefcase and pulled out a file.

'As we are sat here at this moment sixty-six people in Erewash are legally homeless'.

I asked him if that meant that we would go out on the streets that evening and find sixty-six people sleeping rough.

He explained to me what legally homeless meant and his personal view on the situation. He went on to say that many people who are registered would be sleeping on friends' settees as a temporary solution, others would be pushed out to the cities, other would be in derelict buildings, others would be on park benches or sleeping in skips.

I asked him how many beds did we have in Erewash to help such people. He looked at me and said, 'Three at most, but those are not always available'.

The Challenge

We parted company that day, little did I realise that we would be working together again very soon.
I went to West Park and quietly summed up in my mind and heart what I had been told and what I had seen. I asked God, 'why?' and over the coming days I felt the simple answer was 'don't ask why but do something to help'.
After further conversations with a County Council Officer, other church and community groups, I pulled all my findings together to present back to the team leaders' meeting.
It's now early Summer 1995 and I felt as though I had done everything I could at that point.
Through our outreach work on the park we managed to keep in touch with that small group of young men, offering them food and any practical help we could at that point. I got a real sense of

hopelessness as we talked and before long in that early Summer period they disappeared from the park.

None of the other young people seemed to know where they were or what had happened to them.

I wondered if there was more we could have done at that point.

Our youth programme continued with vigour and there was always lots to do.

But I continued asking, knocking, seeking to see if we could do anymore.

Chapter 7 - Fading Summer 1995

Summer 1995 was fast moving to Autumn and at the beginning of September we were about to find out why one of the young men who had been sleeping on the park had disappeared.

The Erewash Housing Officer called me to ask if the church community had managed to make any progress in securing accommodation for the homeless.

I tried to be upbeat with the stories of church members who had already opened their homes to help people with finding accommodation. I told him that my parents were helping two lads in their late teens. They had come to their attention through other family contacts.

I mentioned Graham and Diane and also Maureen, all church members, and the positive help they had been in providing a roof over young people's heads.

I told him of how I admired these people because of their willingness to open their homes and assist, particularly young people in this way. Their example was to prove invaluable in what the Housing Officer was about to say next.

He asked me if I knew someone called Kenny.

I reminded him of the small group of young men on the park and our outreach work.

'Is it the same Kenny?' I asked.

Kenny had been in Nottingham City Hospital Burns Unit for over five weeks. The officer went on.

They can't release Kenny because he has no home to go to.

The story unfolded.

He had sustained horrific injuries after someone had sprayed lighter fluid onto his acrylic Chicago Bulls jacket and set fire to him.

Kenny had sustained 30% burns to the centre of his body due to the burning acrylic clinging to his skin.

I found out later that Kenny's heart had stopped beating for a long period of time but surgeons had managed to save him.

Cheer for victim of fire horror

EXCLUSIVE by Ian Whadcoa

A HOMELESS man who was throw into a skip and set on fire could be on of the first people to move into ne accommodation in a bid to make hi forget his "horrific experience."

The man, known to many people in Lor Eaton and Breaston as Ken, was attacked by vi lains who poured petrol on him and then set hi alight.

He suffered serious burns to his body and had to under extensive skin grafts at Nottingham's City Hospital.

His face escaped injury and he is expected to make a fu recovery. Police are still investigating the "horrendo attack."

Now Ken, who used to wear a red padded all-in-one su is lodging with one of the leaders of the Oasis Christi Centre before moving into new accommodation which w aim to cure Long Eaton's homeless problem.

Minister-in-training at the Oasis Dean Anderson said th the church has had a property donated but had been left wi the task of raising £13,000 to clear the mortgage.

The project could help up to 12 people and Ken wou have a room in the scheme which he would help decor; when he is well enough.

Homeless problem

A number of charity events have already raised a substa tial amount of the money needed — and church officials a confident that they will collect all the cash.

Pastor Anderson said: "Ken has gone through a horri experience and he has got to come to terms with it.

"We've always wanted to help homeless young people a the issues were talked through with the leadership here spread awareness.

"We thought there was a homelessness problem in E wash and this was backed up by statistics supplied by t housing department which confirmed that 16- and 17-ye olds among others were particularly affected.

The project has been welcomed by Erewash Boroug Council as it provides "extra options for young people."

Money is still being collected to pay of the mortgage a the fund was boosted by a donation of £250 from members the Breaston community.

Anyone who wishes to add to the Oasis Trust Fund shou contact the Oasis Christian Centre on (0115) 946 0463.

● Police are still appealing for information regarding t attack on Ken and anyone who can help is being urged to c Long Eaton police on (0115) 946 1101.

New centre for homeless oper

A NEW centre to house the homeless ha been opened in Long Eaton.

Aspire Trust Fund is an organisation commi to helping provide shelter for the homel together with the Oasis Christian Centr Derby Road.

Coun Bill Camm was invited by head (ter of the Oasis Christian Centre, Dean Anderson, to cut the ribbon opening th building in Station Road.

TSB Lloyds Foundation granted the tr £3,000 towards the pr Mr Anderson said: "we have gone all out into the office. It is be out in the community The building has b field and an office for i is not just an office, h and advice."

The office is open fi

A SCHEME which aims to cure Long Eaton's homeless problem is ahead of schedule.

Leaders at the Oasis Christian Centre three planned to buy a property which will give up to 12 homeless people accommoda tion.

And the first of the tenants will start to move into the Aspire Home at the beginning of December — more than a month earlier than expected.

They will include a man who slept on the streets, known as Ken, who was thrown into a skip and had had petrol poured on him before being set on fire by thugs.

Pastor at the Oasis Christian Centre Dean Anderson said: "We've always

By Ian Whadcoat

Aspire Trust Fund and the church have managed to obtain the former Park Farm shop in Long Eaton High Street to use as a fundraising headquarters.

The Aspire Shop, next door to the Christian centre's coffee bar, will open later this month and bring back an old tradition to the town which has dis appeared following the closure of the Co-op. Wool Chain, which will be in its grotto there from November 24 to tacer youngsters.

We weren't in a position as a church community to help, but as I thought more about this dreadful situation I just wondered if.

I arranged to visit Kenny with the Erewash Borough Council Housing Officer and quickly realised why they were so keen to discharge him.

That same evening we sat down for tea as a family and I began to talk about Kenny's plight. Michael, who is now eleven, said that he could share Nathan's bedroom and that Kenny could have his.
I looked at Lynnette and then we said a simple prayer together.
On the 16th September 1995 Kenny came to stay with us.
Michael had moved all his things into Nathan's room and we were ready to welcome our guest.
The stage was set for progression to the beginning of The Aspire Trust that would become The Canaan Trust.

Chapter 8 - Aspire

Our families were supportive in our move but quietly we knew they had concerns. This worked positively in moving up the gears in our progression to set up a house project to assist people who found themselves in this desperate situation.

We worked with local solicitors to set up charitable status for our project and people in the church community and the community in general started to raise funds for the purchase of a property.

There were flower arranging evenings with displays auctioned to raise money.

There were other auctions where people donated anything from a week in a holiday cottage to cleaning cars to tidying gardens.

Fun days were arranged with bouncy castles, BBQ food and, yes, we were put in the stocks and pelted with cold water sponges. You name it, the community did it to raise money.

The church for over a year at this point had been serving coffee and refreshments from a shop in the town centre. Before it had closed it used to be a music shop selling vinyl records, cassettes and other music related items. It was called

The Oasis Music Shop.

Molly and the team would make fresh sandwiches every day and serve with great enthusiasm and always seemingly with a smile. This base, right in the centre of town was invaluable in furthering news about what we were about and helping us raise awareness about the Trust and raising money.

The project was still lacking a name and one particular morning I was walking along Derby Road opposite the church building when it hit me. A spire. The church had a spire and that was what we were doing. We were aspiring to help local people who found themselves homeless. And in turn, with our assistance, they would aspire to see their situation turned around to see a place to live, a place where they could shut the door and lay their head down in security.

The very thing that the majority of us take for granted the homeless aspire to.

So the project affectionately became known as The Aspire Trust.

And that Trust started with trustees who were passionate about seeing that first property up and running as soon as practically possible.

Jill, Gary, Tony, all church members, and myself spearheaded this work along with a whole host of different people who supported us in seeing that dream come to reality in a very short space of time, that three bedroom house right in the centre of Long Eaton and the whole thing coming about in a way that none of us would have even dreamt about.

Mid October 1995 and the money continued coming in but we knew at this point we were still a long way off to buying that first property.

Chapter 9 - The Springboard

Kenny was finding his way with us as a family but the physical and psychological pain of what he had been through was his greatest challenge. We supported him in the best way that we could see he needed, whilst encouraging him to continue with the professional help that was available to him. I worked with him on making sure he didn't miss appointments and gently we built some sort of relationship.

The truth was, at points I did wonder if we had made the right decision but we pressed on.

One particular night, after Kenny had been with us for about a month, he didn't come home. I'd listened for him coming through the front door but by morning we realised that he wasn't in his bedroom. I wondered if he'd had second thoughts about being with us. All his belongings were still there in his room. Michael and Nathan became concerned for him asking where he was and after the second night of him not coming home I decided to notify the police. It was at least another thirty-six hours before we had a phone call to say that Kenny was in the Derbyshire Royal Infirmary. He had been beaten up by a group with baseball bats in the centre of Long Eaton. I straight away drove over to Derby and found the ward where Kenny was.

I looked at him and sobbed. The white sheets seemed to magnify the black and blue bruising around his head. His face was swollen beyond recognition. This young man who just a couple of months before had received 30% burns to the centre of his body was left for dead and now, a second time he had been left for dead.

My tears became angry. How on earth could someone do something as cruel as this?

Kenny's pain was about to catapult the project forward. As he made his way home from the Derbyshire Royal Infirmary, a couple in the church community had offered their house for the Trust to use. It would be its first property to home those who were homeless, to care for those who seemed to be uncared for.

I was keen to find out who had made such a generous offer but I think that I already knew.

My mum and dad had approached Michael and told him that they wanted the church to use their house to progress the work of the Trust. At first I wondered why they hadn't come to me and then I realised that I would have worked overtime to dissuade them from making such a decision.

They told me that down the years and right back to that first help they had received back in 1960 from my Auntie and Uncle they had wanted to help people who found themselves in difficulty when it came to a place to live. They were convinced that this was the right thing for them to do and that they needed to give their home.

Kenny's home was with us for now, but soon, and a lot sooner than any of us imagined he would have a place in The Aspire Trust's first property.

The House

From mid October, with volunteers, trades people and a whole host of visitors offering help, the work quickly progressed as Christmas was now on the winter horizon. Our paint roller trays were seeing those last bits of paint finishing the beginning of a story that had lots more to unfold.

16th December 1995 our first residents moved in. Three young men including Kenny.

Their faces said it all. Now smiling after months and years of heartache and rejection. Positive progression for them and our learning curve continued, steeply at times.

We made every effort to make Christmas special for those young men with all the trimmings.

This was just the beginning of what would be an exciting, challenging journey for this newly established project.

2020 will see twenty-five years of the Trust serving Erewash and the story of those twenty-five years are not all mine to tell.
But what is mine to tell is a story that continues to 1999 and ongoing friendship with Kenny until he passed away in 2007.

Isaiah ch 58 v 6-8
'Is not this the kind of fasting I have chosen: to loose the chains of injustice and untie the cords of the yoke, to set the oppressed free and break every yoke?

Is it not to share your food with the hungry and to provide the poor wanderer with shelter - when you see the naked, to clothe them, and not turn away from your own flesh and blood?

Then your light will break forth like the dawn, and your healing will quickly appear; then your righteousness will go before you, and the glory of the Lord will be your rear guard'.

[From The New International Version of the Bible]

The Office

Progression

Further progression